Everything Moves

Written by Robert Roe and Joshua Hatch
Series Consultant: Linda Hoyt

WorldWise™
Content-based Learning

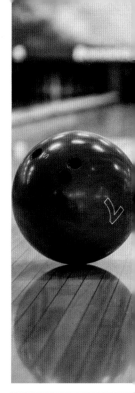

Contents

Introduction

If you look around, what do you see? You see things moving all the time. People walk. Cars drive. Aeroplanes fly. If you throw a ball high up in the air, it will fall back to the ground.

These things happen according to certain rules. But unlike rules your parents ask you to follow — when to wake up, when to go to bed — these rules are the rules of nature. We call these rules physics.

These rules of nature apply to everything. They apply to you, to your friends, to plants, to animals and even to planets and stars.

Forces are the rules of nature that make everything move.

Chapter 1

Making things move

How do things start moving in the first place? If there's a ball on the ground, it won't just move on its own. Something else has to happen to make it move.

You could kick the ball. You could throw the ball. You could hit the ball with a stick. Or you could just pick up the ball. All these things would make the ball move.

Kicking, throwing, hitting and picking up are all ways you can exert force on a ball. These types of forces are called pushing and pulling.

When you kick, throw or hit a ball, that's pushing. You can push a ball with your foot, your hand or with a racquet.

Picking up a ball is a form of pulling. Another form of pulling would be tugging on a rope.

 Try this

Have you ever played play tug-of-war? It's a great way to see a pulling force in action. Get some friends together and find a long piece of rope. Divide your friends into two teams. Have them stand on opposite sides of a line on the ground. Each team grabs an end of the rope and pulls and pulls and pulls. Eventually, one team will pull the other across the line. That team is the winner. It had the stronger pulling force.

Forces in action: Contact and non-contact forces

We know that without forces, nothing moves. There has to be a force from a push or a pull. A ball sitting on a field will stay there unless some force moves it. Maybe a gust of wind will push the ball, or someone will kick it, but without a force, the ball will remain still.

When you push or pull something you touch it with your hand or your foot or something else, such as a bat. You make contact with it.

Pushing and pulling are contact forces.

A kick is one example of a contact force. For a brief moment your foot touches the ball. Your foot slows down a little and the ball speeds up a lot. The harder you kick, the further the ball will go.

Gravity

But some forces work without objects touching each other. These are called non-contact forces.

You experience non-contact forces all of the time.

You can't see **gravity**. You can't smell it. You can't touch or hear it. You definitely can't taste it. Gravity almost seems like magic.

Of course, gravity is not magic. Gravity is just another force, and even though you can't see it, gravity affects almost everything you do. It's one of nature's most basic laws.

Gravity is a force that pulls objects towards each other, even if they're not touching each other. The bigger the object, the more force it exerts.

The earth is much bigger than you, so it pulls you towards it and you don't fly off into space!

 Think about ...

Why aren't you floating in space? Maybe that seems like a silly question. But really think about it. You're not tied to the ground. You don't have magnets on your feet. Yet you're not floating in the air, either. Something is holding you down. What is it? And how does it work? It's **gravity.** Gravity is why people don't float off the earth.

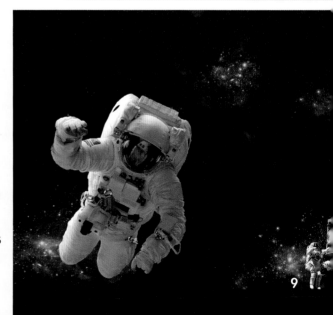

The force of gravity

Here's how you can think about gravity. Imagine standing in the middle of a big trampoline. The trampoline sinks where you're standing. If a friend rolls a tennis ball onto the trampoline, what would it do? Would it roll towards the edge? Or would it rolls toward you?

Of course, it would roll towards you. That's similar to how gravity works. The ball moves downhill because of the force of gravity.

When you push down on the trampoline to jump, you create a force that pushes you up into the air. What is it that slows you down and brings you back again?

How does gravity affect your life? If you play sports, you probably think about gravity a lot, even if you don't know it. If you play basketball, you have to overcome gravity to shoot the ball through the hoop. If you ski, gravity is what pulls you down the mountain (and sometimes makes you fall).

Case study
Thinking like a scientist: Under the apple tree

One fine day in 1665, so the story goes, Isaac Newton sat in the shade of an apple tree behind his mother's house, thinking. By chance he saw an apple fall from the tree. It made him wonder.

Why did the apple fall straight down?

Why not sideways?

Why can't apples fall up?

Scientists in Newton's day didn't understand gravity very well. They explained that apples fell down because they were "earthy" things and their "natural home" was down on Earth. The moon and planets floated in the sky because they were "space" things and liked to stay in space.

Find out more
Isaac Newton lived over 300 years ago and is recognised as one of the most famous scientists of all time. Find out more about Newton's laws of motion.

But this explanation didn't satisfy Newton. He was sure that the universe works by following a few simple rules that are true everywhere — not one rule for apples and another for planets. But what are those rules?

Newton had already figured out that for things to move, they had to feel a force, a push or a pull. Since gravity moves apples, it must be a force too.

The moon and the stars

As he sat under the apple tree, Newton was also thinking about the moon and stars. What keeps the moon moving around the Earth? What keeps the planets in their orbits? Why don't they fly off into space?

Could the same force pulling on the falling apple also pull on the moon? Could Earth's gravity be the mysterious, invisible string that keeps the moon from flying off into space?

There was one problem with this idea. If gravity pulls on the moon with the same force that it pulls on an apple, the moon should come crashing down.

But what if gravity weakens with distance? Newton soon worked out that gravity changes with distance. The pull of gravity gets weaker the further apart two objects are. But it reaches all the way to the moon (and beyond).

Master of the universe

Newton was the first to see that Earth and the moon are connected by gravity.

And he didn't stop there. Jupiter has moons circling around it—so Jupiter must have gravity too. So must the other planets. And the sun — its gravity holds the planets in their orbits.

In fact, Newton went even further. Why just planets? What if everything has gravity — even apples? Now this was a brand new idea!

The more he thought about it, the more Newton was convinced he'd finally found one of the great rules of the universe.

Earth is big — it's made of lots of matter, so it has a strong pull. But the moon is also pulling back on the Earth — less strongly, because the moon is much smaller. Even a falling apple has a tiny gravity, and pulls on the Earth a tiny bit. This was a brand new idea, and Newton was the first to think it.

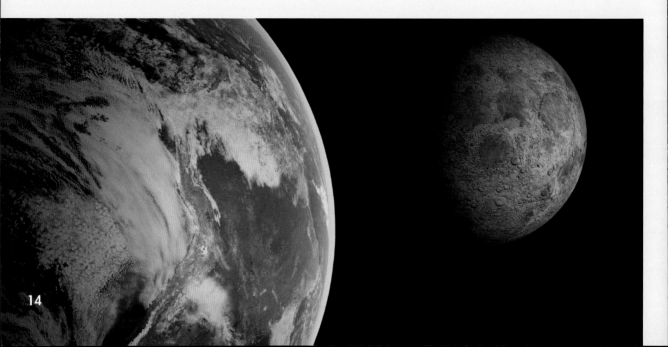

Newton's new explanation of gravity soon solved all sorts of problems that had given scientists headaches for centuries.

It explained why moons orbit planets, and why planets orbit the sun.

It explained why things dropped anywhere on Earth fall in the direction of Earth's centre — that's where most of Earth's mass is.

Newton did not discover gravity (people had noticed it before). But he did work out the rules for how it works. Still, although Newton explained how gravity works, he was never able to explain exactly what it is — though he spent many years trying. In many ways, gravity still remains a great mystery.

Chapter 2

Magnetism

Another non-contact force is magnetism. Once again, it is a force that we cannot see, or touch or smell, but we can see what it does and feel its force.

Do you have any magnets in your house? Maybe on your refrigerator? Magnetism is caused by tiny, invisible charged particles in a metal, usually iron or steel. These tiny particles attract or repel each other. This is called the magnetic field.

You might think magnetism is a contact force, since magnets often snap together. But the force is felt well before the magnets touch. Hold two magnets close to each other, but don't let them touch. Can you feel them being pulled together or pushed apart?

How was magnetism discovered?

The first magnets were not invented, but rather were found in a mineral called magnetite. It is thought that the ancient Greeks were the discoverers of magnetite. There is a story about a shepherd named Magnes whose shoe nails stuck to a rock containing magnetite.

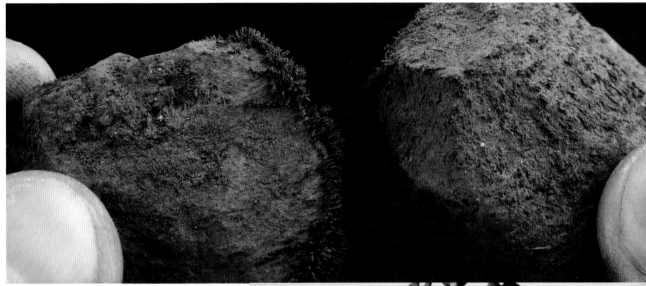

Did you know?
Some magnets are so strong, they can pick up cars. These are called electromagnets and use electric current to generate the magnetic field. You can find electromagnets at junkyards where cranes use them to lift old cars and stack them in big piles.

Earth is also a magnet — a giant one. Earth has a core made of iron that creates a magnetic field all around the planet.

If Earth did not have a magnetic field, there would be no life on this planet. The sun throws off lots of particles into space. If the particles hit Earth, they would be harmful. They would strip away our atmosphere and everything would die. When these particles come towards Earth, our planet's magnetic field acts like a shield.

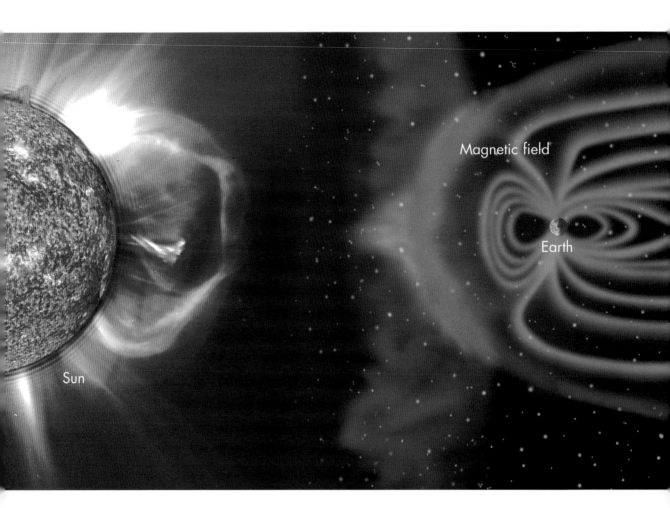

Magnetic field

Earth

Sun

Did you know?
Some animals have magnets in their bodies? Homing pigeons have a magnetic sense that helps them feel Earth's magnetic field. Scientists think that ability helps them find their way.

Compasses

Explorers use magnets to make compasses. No matter where you stand on Earth you can hold a compass in your hand and it will point toward the North Pole. This is an amazingly and very useful thing!

Imagine that you are in the middle of the ocean, and you are looking all around you in every direction and all you can see is water, and it is cloudy so you cannot see the sun... but you have a compass. You can find your direction simply and easily.

Find out more

Why does a compass always point north?

Chapter 3

How friction works

Put your hands together as if you were clapping. Your palms should be touching each other. Keep your hands together. Now slide them back and forth. Go fast! You should feel your palms heating up. Do you know why?

When two objects rub against each other, they cause **friction**. Try rubbing your hands when they are wet. Is that easier or harder? You are reducing friction by making your palms slippery.

Here's a question: If you roll a ball on the ground, will it ever stop rolling? Of course it will. Why? As the ball rolls, it rubs against a surface like grass or concrete, and friction slows the ball until it stops rolling. How quickly the ball stops depends on how much friction there is.

If you roll a ball on a hard, smooth floor or footpath, it might roll for a long time. What if you took that ball outside and rolled it on the grass or sandy beach? Would it go further?

The more friction there is, the sooner the ball will stop.

Here's another example: Is it easier to slide across the gym floor in your shoes or in your socks?

It's a lot easier (and more fun) in your socks, right? That's because your smooth, soft socks create less friction than your hard shoes.

Sailboats and friction

What does friction have to do with sailing a boat? When wind blows, air pushes on the sail and the sailboat moves. At the same time, the sailboat is also rubbing against the water. That's friction!

If the power of the wind pushing on the sail is greater than the friction of the boat rubbing against the water, the sailboat will move. But if the wind is weak, then the friction of the water wins and the sailboat just sits.

Sailboats have smooth **hulls** that are shaped to **glide** through the water as the boat gains speed from the force of the wind. The smoother the hull, the less friction and the more easily the wind can move the boat.

A view of a boat hull from under the water.

23

Sledding and friction

Friction is a funny thing. Sometimes you want a lot of it. Sometimes you want as little as possible.

Let's say you go **sledding** in the snow. Snow is slippery, so it reduces friction. That makes sledding downhill super fun.

But then you have to climb up the hill for another run. The slippery snow has very little friction. This makes it hard for you to use force to push against the snow with your feet as you walk up.

Too little friction means you'll slip and fall. Too much friction and the sled won't slide.

Think about ...

How hard is it to walk up a slide at the playground? It depends on how steep it is and how slippery the surface is. Why is it harder to walk up than to slide down?

25

Chapter 4

Forces working together

Many **forces** can work at the same time. A kicked ball is pushed by your foot at the same time as it is pulled to the earth by **gravity**. As it flies through the air, wind resistance pushes against the ball and slows it down. That's why a kicked ball falls to the ground. As it rolls, the **friction** of the grass against the ball makes it stop. All these forces combined to determine its motion.

Forces can also cancel each other out. You could kick a ball with all your strength, but if the ball weighs as much as a car, it probably won't go anywhere. That's because the ball's gravity and friction are greater than the force of your kick.

Think about …
When you are riding a bicycle, what are the forces acting on you and on the bicycle? Think about the wheels moving on the road.

What is happening here?   What forces are at work?

Gravity is pulling the skydiver down. Air trapped in the open parachute is pushing upward. This is slowing the speed of the parachute and skydiver falling towards the ground. Without the air in the parachute, the skydiver would crash back towards the ground.

Fun with forces: Up, up, up and over!

Roller-coaster cars don't have an engine. So, how do they move?

A big chain pulls them up the first hill. After that, gravity pulls them around the track. On most coasters, the first hill is the tallest. Each after that is a little bit shorter than the last one.

As the cars roll down each hill, they build up enough speed to carry them up and over the next hill. But as the coaster rushes forwards, the wheels rub against the track and the cars push against the air. This rubbing and pushing steal a bit of the cars' energy, so they can get over only a slightly shorter hill next time.

? Did you know?

As a roller-coaster car goes over the top of a hill and starts to **plunge** down, for a second your body is still travelling upwards. This makes you feel like you're floating. This floating sensation is called airtime.

On a good roller-coaster ride, steep climbs and drops are spaced between more gentle hills and turns, to let you catch your breath. To build suspense, some coasters take riders through dark tunnels. And that can be a real thrill — for some people.

Conclusion

A **force** is a push or pull. Nothing moves without a force pushing or pulling it.

We use forces to move objects. You throw a ball by pushing it, and pick it up off the ground by pulling or lifting it.

Gravity is an invisible non-contact force that keeps Earth moving around the sun, and keeps you from flying off into space.

Friction is caused when moving things rub against surfaces and it slows them down. Friction keeps cars from sliding off the road.

Magnetism is caused when tiny particles in a metal, usually iron, attract or repel each other.

Everything moves because of the forces that are all around us.

Glossary

exert to apply onto something

forces pushes or pulls that make things move

friction the amount of resistance an object experiences when moving over another

glide to move in a smooth, continuous way

gravity a force that causes two objects to move towards each other

hull the bottom section of a boat or ship

plunge to quickly dive down

sledding travelling over snow on a flat vehicle that has runners

suspense a feeling of uncertainty about what might happen next

Index